CREDIT AND FUNDING

The Stuff They Don't Teach You in Highschool & College

Visit the author's website at www.carlosdsmith.com

support@creditandfundingbook.com and/or 1-888-676-7333

The information in this book is provided as an information resource only, and does not constitute legal, financial, investment, tax or other advice. Carlos D. Smith and/or Smith Financials LLC gives no warranty and accepts no responsibility or liability for the accuracy or completeness of the information and materials contained in this book. Under no circumstance will Carlos D. Smith and/or Smith Financials LLC be held responsible or liable in any way for any claims, damages, losses, expenses, costs or liabilities whatsoever (including, without limitation, any direct or indirect damages for any personal, business, financial or other losses) resulting or arising directly or indirectly from your use of or inability to use this book or any websites linked to it or in it, or from your reliance on the information and material on this book, even if Carlos D. Smith and/or Smith Financials LLC has been advised of the possibility of such damages in advance.

ISBN-13: 978-1-7372605-0-9 (Epub)
ISBN-13: 978-1-7372605-1-6 (Audio)
ISBN-13: 978-1-7372605-2-3 (Paperback)

Dedication

This book is dedicated to anyone who is trying to improve their financial stability through credit so they can live the life of their dreams.

Carlos refers to Dr. Robert C. Worstell's quote: *"Successful people are not without problems. They're simply people who've learned to solve their problems."*

That is how Carlos sees the world.

To my muse

JEWEL SMITH

Contents

CHAPTER 01

How To Read & Understand Your Credit Report

WHAT'S IN YOUR CREDIT REPORT?

1. **Personal Information**

This includes your name, date of birth, social security number, phone numbers and your current and past addresses. The latter one plays a key role when you start fixing your scores so take note!

Personal Information				
Name(s) associated with your credit				
Name	**Name identification number**			
JON CONSUMER	3055			• Dispute
JONATHAN CONSUMER	25152			• Dispute
J CONSUMER	20726			• Dispute
Address(es) associated with your credit				
Address	**Address identification number**	**Residence type**	**Geographical code**	
1475 MAIN ST ANYTOWN USA 12345-1475	0122937323	Single family	0-70010-17-2520	• Dispute
1036 MAIN ST APT143 ANYTOWN USA 12345-3043	0122868660	Apartment complex	0-1020410-17-2520	• Dispute
Other personal information associated with your credit				
Social Security number variation(s)				
XXX-XX-2538				• Dispute
XXX-XX-1680				• Dispute
Year of birth				
1991				• Dispute
Spouse or co-applicant				
JANE				• Dispute
Notices				
Your date of birth indicates that credit may have been established before age 18.				

Image: Experian

2. **Credit History**

This lists your open and closed accounts, and of course – your payment history. This is not just historical information. It also accounts for a chunk of your credit score. The length of your credit history covers about 15% of your credit score.

FICO® computes this using AAoA or Average Age of Accounts. The formula for that is:

$$\frac{\textbf{Age of Old Accounts + Age of New Accounts}}{\textbf{Total \# of Accounts}}$$

To make it simple, just remember that longer credit history = better for your score.

However, if you're like me and you like to tinker and validate information, you can use this free resource to compute your AAoA: **https://aaoa-calculator.org/**

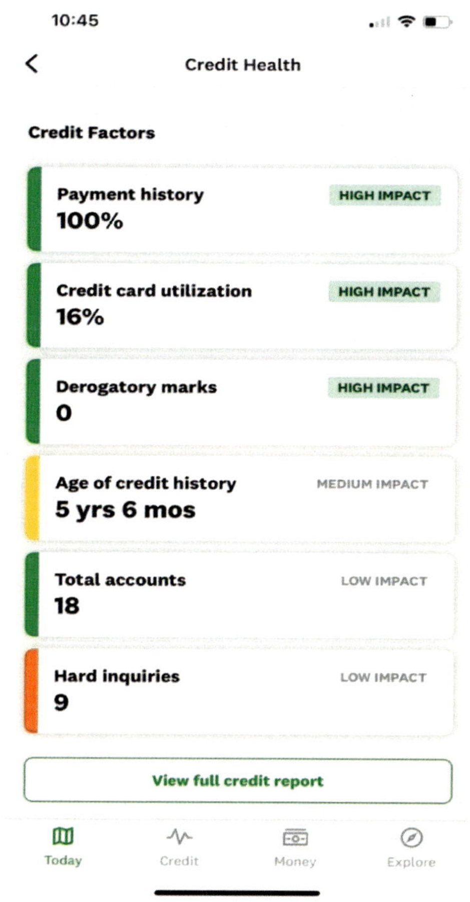

3. Public Records

These are the most stress-inducing items that can appear in your report. These include bankruptcy, judgement, tax liens, lawsuits or even foreclosure and repossessions (in some states).

PUBLIC RECORDS »

FLORIDA FEDERAL COURT - Docket #: XXXXXXXX (PO BOX 559, JACKSONVILLE, FL 32201, (904) 301-6490)

Date Filed:	11/19/2009	Type:	CHAPTER 13 BANKRUPTCY DISMISSED	Court Type:	US Bankruptcy Court
Date Paid:	11/19/2010	Responsibility:	Individual Debt	Plaintiff Attorney:	
Date Updated:	11/19/2009				

Estimated month and year that this item will be removed: 10/2016

4. Credit Inquiries

When an employer, a landlord or any lender requests your credit information from any credit reporting agency, that is called an inquiry.

There are two types of inquiries: hard and soft inquiries. A hard inquiry affects your score, while a soft inquiry does not.

TIP: One or two hard inquiries during loan or credit card applications won't have too much impact on your application. However, six inquiries is getting near the threshold, while nine inquiries will make it very difficult to get approved.

While your credit score is not in your credit report, it is calculated based on the information in your credit report. Credit scores can range from 250, all the way to 900. FICO and the higher VantageScore, the 2 most common credit score providers, use a more narrow range from 300 to 850. Remember that the higher your number, the better your credit.

To get your credit score, request it for free from your financial institution or credit card issuer. You can also pay to get it real-time. Here are some credit monitoring services:

1. Smart Credit: **https://www.smartcredit.com/?PID=56744**
2. Identity IQ: **https://www.identityiq.com/help-you-to-save-money.aspx?offercode=431134U4**
3. Free Annual Credit Report: **https://www.annualcreditreport.com/**

WHAT TO DO WITH ERRORS ON YOUR CREDIT REPORT

When you find errors in your credit report, you can reach out to the creditors and then to the credit agencies. However, I have found more success with disputing directly from the bureaus. If they're unresponsive, you can report the problem to the Consumer Financial Protection Bureau: **https://www.consumerfinance.gov/**.

There are times that you'll see errors that look fraudulent. This can be anything in there that you don't own – for example, a mortgage for a house that isn't yours. In cases like these, I advise you to:

1. Dispute this urgently,
2. File a report with the police, or with the Federal Trade Commission or FTC: **https://www.ftc.gov/**.

GOOD CREDIT REPORT = GOOD DEALS

Good credit gears you up for financial success. It's almost like getting VIP access to life itself – you get approved for loans, and you qualify for better interest rates. You also unlock other perks like credit card rewards which can give you travel deals or even cash back.

YOUR REPORT IS FREE

When you request for it, each of the major credit bureaus must give you a copy of your credit report for free. Yes, that's three, completely free credit reports per year. Take advantage of this to make sure your credit is accurate.

Once again, here's the link to get your free credit report: **https://www.annualcreditreport.com/**

TIP: If you apply for a credit card or loan, and you get declined, you are entitled to a free copy of your report.

Now that you know how to read and use your credit report, you are better prepared to manage your credit.

CHAPTER 02

Credit Scoring Models

Majority of the credit scores used in the US are created by two companies - FICO and VantageScore. FICO is the industry leader, developing their first scoring model in 1989. VantageScore, on the other hand, has been growing significantly since it was created by Equifax, Experian and TransUnion back in 2006.

Both companies state that their scoring model aims to predict how likely a customer will pay a credit obligation 90 days late, or within 2 years. A higher score means you are a safe bet and are most likely to pay your bills on time, while a lower score means the opposite.

Lenders and creditors can choose to use any of the two scoring models to help them determine potential risks with their customers.

Both their scores range from 300 to 850 (although VantageScore only started to adopt FICO's credit range on their 3.0 and 4.0 models).

FICO	
Score Range	***Remarks***
300-579	Very poor
580-669	Fair
670-739	Good
740-799	Very good
800-850	Exceptional
VantageScore	
Score Range	***Remarks***
300-549	Very poor
550-649	Poor
650-699	Fair
700-749	Good
750-850	Excellent

Other differences between the two are:

1. **Score Algorithm**

Although their score ranges are almost similar, their algorithm still vary, as seen below:

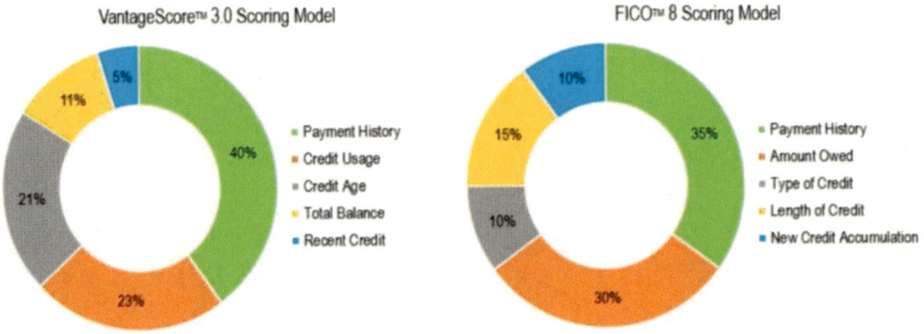

2. **Tri-Bureau VS Bureau-Specific**

Since VantageScore was helmed by Experian, Equifax and TransUnion, it makes sense that their model can be used with a credit report from any of the three bureaus.

FICO, on the other hand, has bureau-specific models. This means that their latest FICO Score 9 has three slightly different models – one for each of the major bureaus.

3. Score Requirements

The minimum requirement for FICO to build your score from your credit reports are:

- Must have a credit account / tradeline that is at least 6 months old,
- Must have activity on any tradeline within the last 6 months, and they don't have to be the same tradelines!

VantageScore, is more lenient, and can build your score if:

- Your credit report has at least one account,
- That account is 6 months old or less

DID YOU KNOW? Deceased consumers will not be scored by either company.

FACTORS AFFECTING YOUR CREDIT SCORES

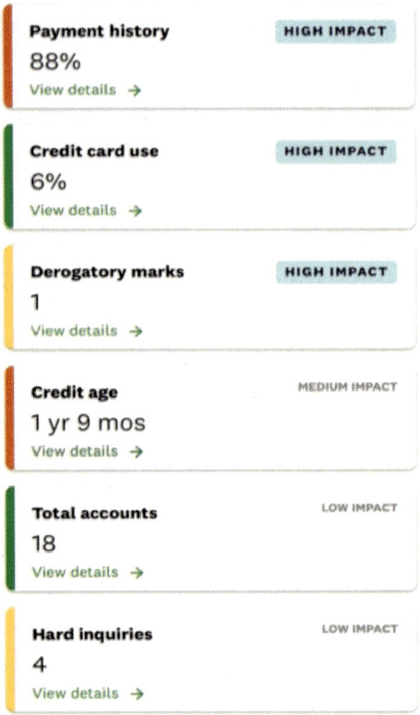

1. Payment History

This is most important component of your credit score, as it immediately gives lenders an idea of your financial habits – can they trust you to pay your loans? How late were you on your payments, and how often or how recently did these happen? Do you have any public records under your name?

Your payment history accounts for 35% of you score.

DID YOU KNOW?

- Paid collection accounts are ignored by FICO 9 & 10, as well as VantageScore 3.0 & 4.0
- Collection accounts with unpaid balance under $100 are ignored by FICO 8 & 9

- Unpaid medical collections have smaller impact on FICO 9 & 10, and VantageScore 4.0

TIP: You have 180 days before any medical debt can negatively impact your credit report. Use this time to settle disputes with your insurance company!

2. Credit Utilization

Under the FICO scoring model, this component looks at how much you owe VS your available revolving credit limits – otherwise called your credit utilization ratio.

A lower utilization is better, although do not make the mistake that having zero balance gives you points – it doesn't. What lenders want to see here is positive activity -- that if get a loan, you can pay it back as timely as possible.

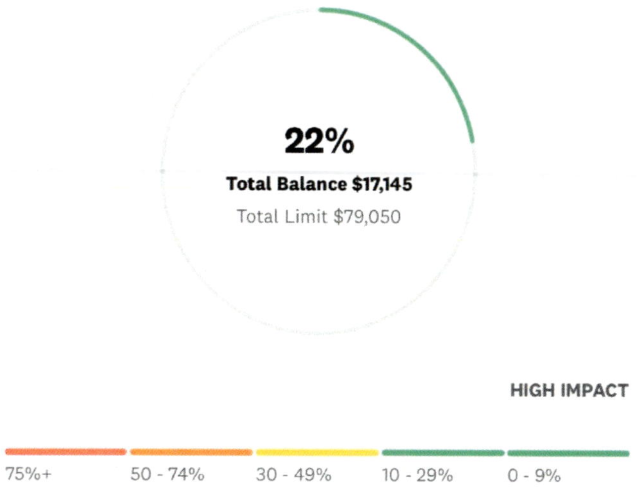

You also don't want to exceed 30% of your credit utilization if you want an excellent credit score. A person with a debt of $100 on a $1,000-limit credit card will always look more financially responsible than a person with a $10,000 credit limit, but with a balance of $9,000.

This component accounts for 30% of your score.

3. Length of Credit History

As I mentioned earlier, a longer credit history is always better as long as you don't have a lot of late payments or other negative items. That doesn't mean that a shorter credit history is automatically bad for you. As long as you always pay your debts responsibly and you don't owe too much, you should be good.

TIP: Never close your credit cards, even if you're not using them. Remember that the age of your positive accounts matters in your overall score.

The age of your credit history takes up 15% of your score.

4. Types of Account

This considers the number of different credit accounts you have on your report. Examples of this are credit cards, student loans, car loans, mortgage, or even store accounts. Maintaining multiple credit products responsibly is a good sign that you can manage your obligations, which is always good for your score.

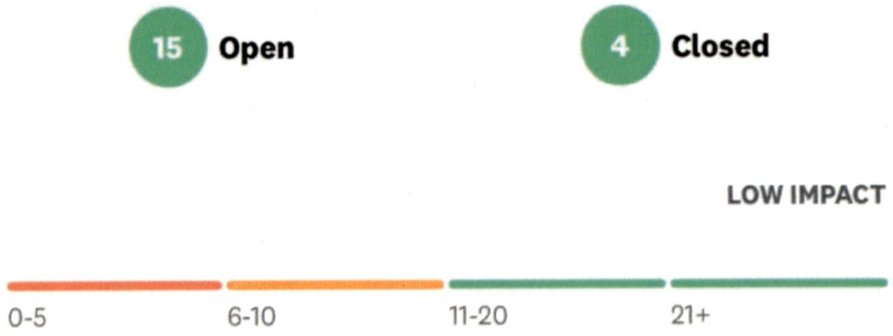

This only amounts to 10% of your total score so don't start opening new accounts just to get this up – which brings us to our final component:

5. **Recent Activity**

Applying for new lines of credit will typically result in lenders doing a hard inquiry (remember from Chapter 1?). The problem here is that too many inquiries signify that you are trying to open lots of new credit – which may imply that you're in a bad financial shape, or that you are getting denied frequently. Whichever the case is, it reflects negatively on your score and would make you a credit risk to lenders.

New credit comprises 10% of your credit score.

TIP: Never close your credit cards, even if you're not using them. Remember that the age of your positive accounts matters in your overall score.

Knowing how FICO and VantageScore creates your credit score is key to understanding how lenders are looking at your data, and more importantly, what you can do to ensure that you look good on paper (which is a reflection of your actual financial situation as well!).

You don't have to bother too much about the differences between the two models. The rule of thumb here is that a good credit history equates to a good credit score. The most basic advice I can give you is to focus on monitoring your credit regularly and be responsible in fulfilling your credit obligations.

As we move to the next chapters, you will learn more about how to further improve your score but always remember the basics because the best solution is still prevention – prevent your score from going down by becoming financially responsible!

CHAPTER 03

Does Personal Information Affect Your Credit Score?

Let's get this out the gate – your personal information does NOT have any impact on your credit scores. Its purpose, however, is to allow credit bureaus to validate your identity. This is why you need to ensure that all your information in there is accurate and up to date.

To give you an idea on what to look out for, let's find out what kind of personal information is included in your report:

1. Name

This is the most obvious, but this can also be the most confusing at first glance. Why do you have multiple "versions" of your name in your report?

Personal Information

3 Names	5 Addresses	2 Employers	3 Other Records

This information is reported to us by you, your creditors and/or other sources. Each source may report your information differently, which may result in variations of your name, address, Social Security number, etc. This is used for identification purposes only and does not factor into your Credit Score.

Names

JAMES AKIN	JAMES M AKIN	JIM AKIN
Name ID #	Name ID #	Name ID #

Source: Experian

Three major reasons:

- If you have married or changed your name, then your maiden name or original name will be included. Makes sense though since you probably have taken up financial obligations under those names in the past.

- A creditor or lender may have misspelled your name while they were running your report.
- You may be a victim of identity theft!

ATTENTION: If a name in your credit report is connected to an account that isn't yours, make it a priority to dispute it. This isn't common and might be a sign of identity theft.

It is important to note that your credit data can be mixed up accidentally, most especially if:

- You have a very common name
- You share the same name and birthday as someone else
- You share the same name with your parent or child

Credit mix-ups can lead to inaccuracies in your credit report and if you get mixed up with a person who has poor credit history, it will lower your score.

I know what you're thinking -- if this is the case, then getting mixed up with someone who has good credit history can be good right? Wrong. Any extras in your credit report (even if in good standing) can easily increase your debt-to-income ratio, which can get you denied on your next loan.

2. **Address**

Any residence you've had in the past where you've received bills is potentially listed in your credit report. This is because creditors update your personal information with the bureaus. This means that if you keep your mailing address updated with your creditors, then you can be sure that it will appear in your credit report – although sometimes it takes one or two billing cycles to reflect depending on your creditor.

ATTENTION: Similar to your name, it's possible for wrong addresses to appear in your report. If you see an address that you don't recognize, you may be a victim of identity theft.

As a final note, remember that your addresses will never fall off on its own in your credit report so a historical information of your past residences (where bills are addressed to) will be listed in there. This is especially useful if your job or credit card applications ask for your previous 2-3 addresses to validate your identity.

3. **Social Security Number**

Expect this section to be obscured to prevent identity theft.

4. **Date of Birth**
5. **Spouse' First Name**
6. **Employers**

This may or may not contain your entire employment history since not all employers provide your information to the credit bureaus.

7. **Telephone Numbers**
8. **Consumer Statement**

This is a 100-word written statement (200, if you're in Maine) that you can add in your credit report. You can write this statement yourself and it stays on your report and can be viewed by lenders or creditors unless you remove it.

What does it do? A consumer statement allows you to comment on your negative items and explain your side of the story. It's 100 words though so be concise. This statement is meant to give assurance to lenders that – yes, you have encountered some hardships (due to an extreme medical illness, for example), but you have regained stability and have started to make regular payments again.

This is a privilege afforded to us by the Fair Credit Reporting Act. However, this should be used wisely so as not to further damage your reputation to businesses viewing your report. Creating alibi statements for any delinquencies in your report will not put you in good light and will almost always backfire. You don't want to write that you missed a couple of payments because you went to Maldives for the summer.

Note that a consumer statement is not a magical solution to your negative accounts. In this day and age, a lot of things are automated so expect that machines will not be able to read your consumer statement. Besides, even if lenders see your statement, there is no guarantee that they'll consider it, or even read it.

Another thing to consider here is that if you've added a consumer statement on a negative account and that account gets removed or falls off your report naturally, then you have just flagged yourself that you've had problems in the past which doesn't sit well with lenders.

9. Date Reported

This is the date when your creditor initially reported the information to the bureau.

10. Last Updated

This is the date when your creditor last updated the information to the bureau.

TIPS:

1. If you are a victim of identity theft, **go to Chapter 9**.
2. If you want to submit a consumer statement:
   - ✓ File a formal dispute to the bureaus first. You don't have to write a consumer statement if you can have it removed, right? You only want to write a consumer statement for items that are taking too long to remove or those you can't remove at all. To file a dispute, go to **Chapter 4**.
   - ✓ Write your statement.
   - ✓ Submit your statement:
     - Equifax: **https://www.equifax.com/personal/help/add-consumer-statement-equifax-credit-report/**
     - Experian: **https://www.experian.com/disputes/main.html**
     - TransUnion: **https://service.transunion.com/dss/login.page?dest=dispute**

ATTENTION: Make sure to follow any website instructions since they may have moved pages or links from the time this book was published.

Educating yourself makes all difference if you want to take charge of your financial life. Doing it yourself can be very rewarding but know that there are services available if you don't have the time for it – you will just need to scrutinize and make sure that you are choosing the right partner.

CHAPTER 04

How To Dispute Negative Accounts

Based on what we've tackled so far, you should now be aware that your credit report can contain inaccuracies. The last chapter just taught you how to deal with incorrect personal information and ways to secure it. Now, we'll talk about the rest of the credit errors and ways to FIX them. Before we proceed, grab a copy of your credit report from the three bureaus. Once you have those in hand, go over the steps below:

STEP 1: ITEMS TO CHECK ON YOUR CREDIT REPORT

1. Account Number
2. Balance
3. Date Opened
4. Account Status
5. Payment Status
6. Credit Limit
7. High Balance

Once you've run through these items, go to the next step to know what should be on a look out for.

STEP 2: IDENTIFY CREDIT REPORT ERRORS

The ones listed here impact your scores negatively. Note that some of the items in this list also appear in the last chapter:

1. Incorrect account numbers
2. Accounts that you don't recognize (or not yours to begin with)
3. Incorrect account status
4. Negative accounts that should have fallen off due to age (majority of derogatory accounts must be removed after 7 years)
5. Incorrect addresses (as discussed in Chapter 3)
6. Ex-spouse listed on your loan, or vice-versa – ex-spouse' debt appearing on your report

STEP 3: COLLECT DOCUMENTATION TO VALIDATE YOUR DISPUTES

Your objective here is to convince the investigators that your complaint is valid. Some of the common supporting documentation that you will need are <u>COPIES OF</u>:

- Credit card statements
- Loan documents
- Birth / death certificates
- Divorce documents
- FTC complaint (for Identity Theft only)
- Police report (for Identity Theft only)
- Proof of identity
- Social security number
- Date of birth
- Government-issued ID (e.g. passport or driver's license)

- Proof of address and past addresses (as far back as 2 years)
- Utility bill addressed to you and your current residence

STEP 4: UPDATE YOUR PERSONAL INFORMATION & REMOVE OLD ADDRESSES

Before you go ahead and start your disputes, make sure you fix your personal and remove your old addresses.

Make sure you to include your social security number, government-issued ID and proof of address (utility bill addressed to your current residence). These are part of the documents you should've prepared in the previous step.

To dispute your personal information, use the **File Update Letter** in Chapter 11.

STEP 5: SUBMIT YOUR DISPUTE LETTER

You will need to write your own dispute letter. The technique is to make it as detailed as possible, summarizing all the inaccuracies you have found.

After that, you will need to send the same letter to each credit bureau if the inaccurate/negative information is appearing on all three bureaus. Don't forget to address them to each bureau if you're copy-pasting these letters!

Here are the addresses for each bureau:

- **Equifax**

  Equifax, P.O. Box 740256, Atlanta, GA 30374-0256
- **Experian**

Experian National Consumer Assistance Center, P.O. Box 4500, Allen, TX 75013

- **TransUnion**

  TransUnion LLC, Consumer Dispute Center, P.O. Box 2000, Chester, PA 19016

You might be thinking about online disputes – and I purposely left that out. Yes, those are convenient, but when disputing online – you won't have proof of what you disputed, or that you even submitted one. Another downside is that their websites have disclaimers and waivers that you have to agree with before you can send your disputes. These waivers will put you at a disadvantage since these are meant as protection for them, not you. Not having all the necessary documentation means you won't be able to hold up in court if it comes to a lawsuit.

Disputing via certified mail, on the other hand, gives you proof of WHAT exactly you sent, WHEN you sent it, and WHEN they received it. That means you will also have evidence if they fail to respond or investigate your dispute.

TIP: Make sure to use certified mail so you get proof of mailing and a signature from the recipient. It might cost extra, but it's assurance that the bureaus got what you've sent and are required to take action.

Once the bureaus receive your letters, they would need to complete their investigation within 30-45 days.

TIP: You can grab a 605B, 609 or 611 dispute letter template in **Chapter 11**.

ATTENTION: The act of filing a dispute, by itself, does not hurt your score. However, any changes resulting from your disputes could change your score once those disputes are processed.

There are other options for getting your negative items from your report. Below are some of the methods you can look into.

OPTION 1: SEND A GOODWILL LETTER

If you don't have errors in your report, but want to have some late payments removed – this is an option.

A goodwill letter is simply a letter of forgiveness that you send to your creditor, explaining to them the reason for your negative mark (like missing a payment because of an emergency), and then asking them to consider removing it.

Again – this isn't a letter to the bureau, but a letter directly to your creditor. You are asking your creditor to remove a VALID negative entry as an act of "goodwill."

Note that creditors can deny your request because they have a legal obligation to report your history accurately to the bureaus.

You'll want to use this method if you have a strong credit history and consistent on-time payments, but got into some unfortunate situations like:

- Missing a payment due to unemployment or divorce
- Missing a payment because of a medical emergency where you or a family member got hospitalized

- Missing a payment because of technical issue with a platform you're using, e.g. autopay
- Missing a payment because you moved and didn't get your bill at the new address

Similar to disputes, you'll want to include proof to support your letter. An example is a medical bill from when you were hospitalized.

OPTION 2: SEND A 'PAY FOR DELETE' LETTER

Think of this as negotiating with your lenders and collection agencies. This method involves you writing your creditor to have negative marks removed from your report in exchange for your payment.

A general rule here is that your offer should be higher than what the collection agency paid for your debt, otherwise, why would they even consider it? It has to be beneficial for them to justify removing the record from the bureaus. Negotiating to pay the full amount of the debt will be your best option here since collection agencies buy your debt for only a percentage of your balance due – so this is already profit for them.

Once you've sent your letter, be prepared to negotiate with either the creditor or collection agency over the phone.

Note that majority of creditors like banks don't give you this option, but this strategy could work with smaller companies.

TIP: This method is legal so make sure to get your agreement in writing before you pay. Collection agencies, in particular, tend to have short term memories unless you owe them money, so it's best to have the written agreement in hand before paying.

OPTION 3: GET HELP FROM A PROFESSIONAL

What if your dispute gets rejected or ignored? Or what if you're too busy to write letters, send them, and monitor them every single month?

This is where credit repair / coaching starts to make sense.

My company, Smith Financials LLC, has over 26 years of experience in the financial sector. We've been helping thousands of people with their credit. We also have a network of partners and affiliates that can help you out once your scores are fixed.

Think of credit repair as an alley-oop. It requires precision and teamwork from both parties. I'll line up the shot for you – giving you the perfect opportunity to score – and you take that ball and dunk it home.

Our service can clean your report up and line you up for success, but once we hand your results to you, you will have to maintain the work we have done. The good thing about our service is that we offer what other credit repair companies don't: education.

To learn more about our services, go to our website and book your free consultation: **https://www.smithfinancialsllc.com/freecon**.

CHAPTER 05

Six Other Bureaus You Should Know About

I know what you're thinking – and yes, these are legit credit reporting agencies. They are less well-known than the big three of Equifax, Experian and TransUnion, but that doesn't mean you can ignore them.

When you're dealing with credit, you deal with all credit reporting agencies.

These smaller agencies do the same thing as the major ones – they sell consumer information to creditors and lenders, or just about any business that needs to look at your credit worthiness. Lenders will usually be affiliated with one or more reporting agencies so in case one doesn't respond, they can go to the next one. These six are part of that circle.

One good thing is that these six smaller credit bureaus are covered by the Fair Credit Reporting Act, so everything that applies to the 3 major bureaus, apply to these smaller ones. That includes giving you the right to dispute and correct any inaccuracies on their credit reports, and giving you access to a free credit report each year.

INNOVIS

Innovis is generally referred to as the "fourth credit bureau" and is being used for consumer credit checks by a lot of organizations. Their objective leans more towards identity verification and fraud prevention, and credit reporting services but you can treat them just like any of the big three.

- To request for your Innovis credit report, go to **https://www.innovis.com/personal/creditReport**
- To submit a freeze request, go to **https://www.innovis.com/securityFreeze/index**

SAGESTREAM

- To request for your SageStream credit report, go to **https://forms.sagestreamllc.com/#/consumer-report-self**
- To submit a freeze request, go to **https://www.sagestreamllc.com/security-freeze/**

ADVANCED RESOLUTION SERVICES, INC (ARS)

- To submit a freeze request, go to **https://www.ars-consumeroffice.com/securityfreeze.faces**

LEXISNEXIS RISK SOLUTIONS

- To request for your LexisNexis credit report, go to **https://consumer.risk.lexisnexis.com/request**
- To submit a freeze request, send out your request letter at: LexisNexis Consumer Center, P.O. Box 105108, Atlanta, Georgia, 30348-5108

CORELOGIC CREDCO

- To request for your CredCo credit report or to submit a freeze request, go to **https://www.corelogic.com/solutions/credco-consumer-assistance.aspx**

LCI

This bureau is TransUnion's official bankruptcy public record information provider as of December 1, 2018. This means that some of your requests to LCI are handled by TransUnion as you will see from the link I provided below.

- For credit report inquiries, freeze requests or bankruptcy-related concerns, visit their website for detailed instructions: **https://www.lciinc.com/transunionconsumers/**

TIP: If you're planning to submit a written request for security freeze on any of the bureaus listed above, make sure to include the following information in your letter:

- First and last name
- Social security number
- Date of birth
- Primary phone number
- Address including ZIP code
- Two of the following forms of identification:
    - A copy of a state-issued driver's license or state identification card.

- A copy of a "recent" cable, utility, or phone statement with an address matching the address provided in Step 1. "Recent" is defined as no more than 60 days old from the date of IDA, Inc's receipt of a written request.
- A copy of an SSN card.

TIP: You can grab a **Freeze Request** template in Chapter 11.

TIP: If you want to improve your chances of getting approved for a US Bank credit card, request a security freeze from both SageStream and ARS. US Bank uses both providers and will still approve you even if they can't access those reports.

CHAPTER 06

The Quickest Way To Build Positive Credit

A good credit score can get you anywhere. That's a fact. It's like unlocking a whole new level in your financial life. While getting to that point is a journey on its own, I have compiled helpful tips that can get you there as quickly as possible.

1. Pay your bills on time

Since payment history accounts for the biggest chunk of your credit score, paying your bills on time is the most effective strategy to getting your score in shape. Treat this as a short-term monthly goal.

In case you miss a payment within 30 days, reach out to your creditor, negotiate if you can pay up immediately and ask them to consider not reporting to the late payment to the bureaus.

Lastly, avoid becoming delinquent. Once debt collection is added to your report, it can be hard to remove.

2. Get credit for paying on time

Experian offers to improve your FICO score for free when you use their offering called Experian Boost. This applies to utility, telecom and even streaming services. If you are paying bills on time, you will want to take advantage of this option.

To enroll, link your bank account to Experian Boost (the one you're using to pay bills). After that, you can select the entry (positive, of course!) from your credit history that you want to add to your Experian credit file. And that's it – you get your score increase instantly.

Check it at **https://www.experian.com/consumer-products/score-boost.html**.

Note that recurring payments and utility bill payments are not usually reported to the credit bureaus (unless you become delinquent!) so if you are concerned about signing away more of your personal data to corporations, this might not be for you.

ATTENTION: According to Experian, this offer applies to FICO Score 8 only so if a lender uses another scoring model, you won't see that increase in there.

3. Autopay is your friend

If you're having trouble keeping track of your bills, enroll in autopay. You even have the option to set it up so you only pay the minimum.

Autopay withdraws automatically from your bank account so this can be a lifesaver if you want to maintain a clean payment history. Some companies even offer perks, such as discounts on your interest rates, if you go for autopay.

4. Subscribe to reminders

An alternative to autopay is to set up a payment reminder. Banks and credit card providers usually have an option to send you email reminders, or even push notifications on your devices.

If your provider doesn't have these options, you can always set up a reminder on your phone. You can do what works for you – the important thing is you pay on time.

5. Don't apply for too many accounts at once

As we discussed in the previous chapters, applying for new accounts or any financial products will lead to hard inquiries. These inquiries can easily build up if you're sending out too many credit applications, and as you know by now – leads to a decrease in your score.

There are exceptions here, however, as FICO and VantageScore both have come up with ways to not penalize consumers who are shopping for fair rates.

Multiple hard inquiries related to mortgage, auto loan or student loan applications within a period of 45 days will be counted as a single inquiry by FICO. With VantageScore it's the same, but within a period of 14 days only.

Keep these in mind the next time you start shopping for rates so you can proactively secure your good credit standing.

TIP: In the market for a new card? Majority of credit card companies have pre-qualification forms on their website. If you're not sure that you'll qualify, submit one instead of applying directly as it won't impact your score.

6. Monitor your credit utilization ratio

Your credit utilization ratio is your total credit card balance divided by your total credit limit. Like we discussed in Chapter 2, you will need to aim for below 30% to maintain a good score.

If you find yourself going beyond 30% and you can consistently pay your bills on time (or even in full!), I suggest that you reach out to your credit card provider and ask for a credit increase to lower your utilization.

However, if you're beyond 30% and struggling to pay your bills – you will need to find ways to cut back on your expenses.

7. Leave your oldest accounts open

Remember that the age of your credit history accounts for 15% of your credit score so I'm just repeating it here: Never close your credit cards even if you're not using them. They can passively help boost your score.

8. Get added as an authorized user

An authorized user is a secondary card holder on another person's credit card account. This means you get your own card linked to the original cardholder's account.

This only works if the primary cardholder has a good credit score since you'll technically be inheriting that account's history so it can be calculated into your score.

As an authorized user, you don't have to pay your bills – that still falls under the primary cardholder's responsibilities – which means you have to be careful with your credit card usage and plan out your payments with the primary cardholder.

9. Dispute credit report errors

This can be one of the more powerful ways to build your score if you have lots of inaccuracies in your credit report, but it can also be the most cumbersome to accomplish. You have to be proactive in monitoring your report, and meticulous when dealing with errors (since you need to list them, create letters, mail them and monitor them again). The process will test your patience but when it works, it's rewarding.

Again, you don't have to do this alone. You can always hire professionals if you need to get the job done quickly and accurately.

TIP: If your score is in the 500-600 range, a product called UltraFICO will apply to you. Like Experian Boost, it connects to your bank or savings account. The difference is that UltraFICO uses the information it captures to supplement your current FICO score. Some of the information it captures are your savings, the age of your accounts and how active they are.

Let's say that your score isn't enough to qualify for a loan – any lender using UltraFICO can pull up your UltraFICO score instead provided that your score is only a few points below their requirements. This entire process is considered a single inquiry, which is another good thing.

Let's do a run down on who will benefit the most, and who qualifies for UltraFICO:

- People with scores within the upper 500s to lower 600s
- People with thin credit history
- People trying to rebuild their credit
- Those with $400 or more in their savings account
- Those without a negative account balance in the past 3 months

If you're interested, check it at https://www.fico.com/ultrafico/.

ATTENTION: UltraFICO only applies if the lender is using an Experian credit score.

CHAPTER 07

How To Effectively Build Your Child's Credit

But getting a credit card starts at 18! True, but that doesn't mean you can't lay out the groundwork. Credit education doesn't have to be complex. As a parent, you can be creative in figuring out ways of getting their head in the game.

Let's start with the most obvious.

1. **Start their education early**

The key here is to involve them in financial routines. Doing your bills? Explain to them why you have to do it, and how it helps your family in return. Considering if a PlayStation 5 is a worthy purchase? Be honest and tell them why you're still thinking about it, and how you're planning to pay for it.

Let them understand the concept of money – where it comes from, how you spend it, and why it helps to have it on hand.

If your child is a young adult, they most likely understand borrowing money and paying it off, so this is the best time to explain how debt and credit work.

You won't get your kids excited about credit scores yet, but if you make these topics a part of your daily conversations, it will eventually stick.

2. **Put the learning to practical use**

If you're teaching your child about the concept of money, try getting them to save some of their allowance so if there's something they really want, they have money to buy it. Put the theories into practice.

Let's say that they really want something, and their savings is not enough, you can offer to shoulder the remaining balance, and they can pay it back (by doing some weekly chores, for example – you can be creative!). This teaches them the value of money early on, and the importance of working for the things they want.

3. **Add your child as an authorized user**

In the previous chapter, we talked about how becoming an authorized user can help boost your credit score. This is one practical application of that topic. Since your kid can't get credit cards yet, you can simply add them as secondary cardholders. This way, they get the benefit of your good credit history.

Talk to your credit card provider about the minimum age requirements and confirm with them if your secondary cardholder's activity is reported to the bureaus.

Once they get their first billing statement, walk them through it. Help them understand the consequences if they don't pay on time and how that impacts their future – I mean really dig into the reality of it.

4. **Get them to report their credit**

Remember Experian Boost and UltraFICO from the last chapter? Those are most beneficial for people with thin credit histories – and yes, you guessed right – that applies to your child. With newer offerings such as these, your child gets the necessary boost to help them build credit.

To do this, your child needs to have a utility bill under their name. When they turn 18, and they start to open their own phone or internet account, encourage them to subscribe to those 2 services so all their payments will then be reported to the bureaus.

This also gives them a better sense of responsibility since you're already involving them in the credit game.

5. **Co-sign your child's loan**

I put this last since there are inherent risks involved here and if your child mishandles their obligation, it could put a strain on your family relationship and on your own credit score.

But considering the best-case scenario, and that your child understands their responsibilities in this endeavor – this can be another avenue to help them build credit without a credit card especially since a mix of different types of credit accounts takes up 10% of your score (you go back to Chapter 2 if you need a refresher on your score components!).

Note that you don't have to limit yourself to my suggestions. If you have an approach that you think can work – go for it. At the end of the day, your objective here is to prepare your child for the real world. You want them to experience mistakes early on, rather than late in life when the stakes are higher, and they already have families to support. These are our kids we're talking about here after all – we want them to succeed in life and do better than us in some or all aspects of life.

CHAPTER 08

The Truth About Tradelines

If you've been going around trying to fix your credit, you may have heard of tradelines. To those of you who's new to this, a tradeline is simply an account on your credit report. If it's just an entry in your report, you might be asking yourself, "then what's the buzz about?"

To answer that, let's go back on a previous topic in **Chapter 7**. Remember when we talked about adding your child as an authorized user to help boost their credit? The concept of buying tradelines revolve around that.

To recap – when you add your child as an authorized user on your account, they get the benefit of your account's history (if it's a positive history!). Now, there are people with excellent credit scores who are offering to "rent out" their seasoned tradelines (or simply, accounts with an established positive history) in exchange for payment.

Yes, you heard that right. By having these tradelines on your report, you get a boost on your credit score.

Is this practice illegal? No, it's not illegal since adding secondary cardholders to your account is legal. It's an accepted strategy to add your spouse or your kid as authorize users so they can benefit from your positive score.

Although it's not illegal, buying tradelines can be viewed as dishonest. Creditors want to make fair decisions based on your credit history and by buying tradelines, you are claiming to be credit worthy when you otherwise wouldn't be.

This boils down to your perspective, because you might argue that by adding your kid as an authorized user – you are lending them your credit worthiness as well. What makes a third party's credit history any different, right? Whether you buy it or you got it from a family member, it is meant to do the same thing.

If you're not interested in tradelines, you can skip to the next chapter. But if you're still reading, let's dive in to how you can leverage tradelines in your overall credit strategy.

HOW TO USE TRADELINES EFFECTIVELY

It's important to note that tradelines can stay in your account for as little as 45 days up to as long as 7 years. You can also get decreasing benefits each month that it stays on your account. Because of this, you want to take advantage of the boost immediately.

If you're in the market for a house, make sure you have everything in order – your finances, prep work, mortgage application, documents – after that, add the tradelines (your final step!), and watch everything fall into place.

TIP: If you want to know more about the inner workings of buying tradelines, you can read about it online, or simply follow me on social media so we can talk about these topics!

COMMON MISTAKES WHEN BUYING TRADELINES

1. **Having the wrong expectations**

If you don't have any idea on how tradelines work, then you might be wasting money by going this route. For example, if you think tradelines can repair your credit, think again. Remember from Chapter 1 that there are 5 components that make up your credit score so it's best to build around that.

Apart from that, having negative accounts in your credit report also drag your score down and getting new tradelines simply won't solve that. You will be better off getting your credit repaired first.

You can reach out to tradeline companies to get more guidance and how tradelines can help you with your particular goals.

2. Adding tradelines while you have freezes or fraud alerts

Freezes and fraud alerts lock your account so nothing gets posted on your credit report, including tradelines.

You can contact the bureaus to have these lifted before you decide to purchase new tradelines. Don't make an expensive mistake!

3. Not understanding the age factor of tradelines

Tradelines can only be effective depending on the existing items in your credit report. Let's say that the average age of your accounts is 12 years. If you get an 8-year-old tradeline, don't be surprised if it doesn't give you the best result since it is way lower than your existing 12-year-old average.

But try adding that 8-year-old tradeline in an account that's only 1 or 2 years old? Now we're talking! Expect to see more impactful results in that scenario.

4. Age vs Limit

Personally, I think age is a more powerful metric to gauge a tradeline's effectivity but each credit report is unique so it's best to consider both when purchasing your tradelines.

Make sure to get an assessment from a tradeline company so they can help assess your situation and determine what's best for you.

5. Testing

It's not uncommon for people to test something out – and oftentimes, they will end up buying a cheap tradeline to see if it works for them. First off, cheap tradelines have less age. Secondly, buying 1, then 2 then 3 is not always the wisest strategy since there is more to tradelines than just dumping them randomly in your report.

You need to know how your credit report and its components look like to know what you need. This is why it's best to reach out to a tradeline company first so they can assist you in figuring out what's right for you based on the status of your report and the goals you have in mind.

6. Buying from unreputable companies

Do you know what's worse than a low-quality tradeline? One that you purchased at a higher price, then did not post.

There are a lot of tradeline companies popping up online and it can be hard for consumers to figure out who to trust. Here are a couple of red flags to see if a company's no good:

- Their website doesn't look professional
- Their website isn't secure. See if they start their website with "https"
- Unresponsive customer service
- They have no reviews, or fake reviews

TIP: I'm listing here my top 3 tradeline providers to help you steer clear of unethical tradeline companies:

1. **Tradeline Masters**

They are quite expensive, but you pay for quality here. They are dependable and their technology is user-friendly so it's easy to purchase and understand when your tradeline will post.

Website: **https://tradelinemasters.net/**

2. **BnB Financials**

If you want good prices on tradelines, this is the company for you. Don't be deceived by their lackluster website though – what they lack in technology, they more than make up for in customer service. They are best in class in that regard and can make your journey with them easier.

Website: **http://bnbfinancials.com/**

3. **Superior Tradelines**

This is a good company if you are a beginner at buying tradelines. Their prices are great and their fees are set from $700-$900. If I have one problem with them, it's that their list is hard to read. Apart from that, they can be a good partner.

Website: **https://superiortradelines.com/**

CHAPTER 09

How To Protect Your Credit From Identity Theft

This chapter aims to help you prevent identity theft. Those who have been victims will know how stressful it can be to fix this situation -- imagine spending time and money to prove you're a victim, not to mention gathering what exactly was compromised, then taking steps to recover your identity.

It's an unpleasant experience, and that's exactly why I dedicated an entire chapter to this topic.

While there is no 100% prevention with identity theft since some factors are not in your hands, this chapter aims to help you minimize the risks of you getting targeted.

TIP: You may want to visit the Federal Trade Commission's identity theft website to check for warning signs if someone has stolen your information. You can read more at https://www.identitytheft.gov/warning-signs-of-identity-theft.

HOW TO PREVENT IDENTITY THEFT

1. **Secure your devices**

Put a password on your smartphone, tablet and laptop. Our devices these days house a lot more than just personal information. All the apps living inside your smartphone can be a gateway to your entire personal and financial life.

While we're on the topic of passwords, make sure to use different ones for each account. That way, if you do get compromised on one account, it's harder to breach the rest. Password managers are even available online to help you remember every single one.

If your device has biometric security features like voice, facial or fingerprint recognition – use them!

2. Know what phishing is and how to avoid it

When an email, link or website is made to appear like they're coming from one of your trusted providers (bank, credit card provider, lender, etc.) – this is called phishing.

Sometimes it's a link that takes you to a fake version of your website with the intention of getting your account information, or even an attachment that installs a malware on your device once you open it. Thieves can get really creative and sophisticated with their methods so it's best to keep yourself updated.

A general rule here is if it looks suspicious, don't open it. When in doubt, call your provider and ask them about the links, SMS or emails you're receiving to see if those are really coming from them.

3. Fraud alerts and freezes

We tackled both of these several times in this book, but let's repeat a vital piece of information here: Adding a fraud alert or a freeze on your credit report will lock it, making it hard for anyone to get to your information, including thieves.

One thing to note is that you can always unfreeze your account if you're applying for new accounts (since creditors will need to look at your report).

This can be an inconvenient way to protect your account, but to me, it's worth the price of prevention.

To find out how to request for fraud alerts and freezes, go to the end of this chapter.

4. Secure your mail or any personal document

Your mailbox can be an easy target for identity thieves. Any sensitive parchment you receive through mail can contain information that's useful to these scammers.

One suggestion is to go for electronic billing statements instead to limit the physical mail you have to receive. You can also shred your receipts before you throw them in the trash.

TIP: If you get pre-approved credit card offers, make sure to get it off your mailbox immediately as it can be used by crooks to open an account. If you want to go a step further, you can even stop getting these offers by opting out at https://www.optoutprescreen.com/, or by calling them at 888-567-8688. This should stop majority of offers, and it's also free.

5. Monitor your accounts

Going back to technology – it's now very easy to get online access to your accounts. Majority of providers offer this option so once you sign up, you can check your statements for suspicious activity real-time.

HOW TO HANDLE IDENTITY THEFT

The key here is to act fast. I suggest the following actions:

1. Report the incident to your creditors and to one of the bureaus (that bureau will report it to the other two).
2. File a report at the FTC's identity theft website, at **https://www.identitytheft.gov/**
3. File a police report.
    - Note that this can be optional unless you have the identity of the thief, or your creditors require you to file one.
4. Put an extended fraud alert on your account.
    - Note that this requires documentation from step 2 and/or step 3.
5. Put a security freeze on your account to prevent further damage.

To request for fraud alerts and freezes, you may contact the bureaus:

- **Equifax**
  Equifax.com/personal/credit-report-services
  800-685-1111

- **Experian**
  Experian.com/help
  888-EXPERIAN (888-397-3742)

- **Transunion**
  TransUnion.com/credit-help
  888-909-8872

CHAPTER 10

Advantages of Good Credit

A good credit score can get you anywhere. That's pretty much a given. One of my objectives in this book is to get you to the point where you can enjoy these perks – to make financial success accessible to everyone. Majority of what's in this chapter will be common knowledge to some of you, but I want you to take this as a motivation of what's on the other side. If you're still working to build your credit, I hope this chapter keeps you going.

1. **Best credit cards**

Anything ranging from having the lowest interest rates, to the best reward packages – you get access to the top products in the market.

Note that most premium cards require a minimum of 700-750 credit score, which can be achievable if you are willing to put in the work.

2. **Best interest rates**

Paying less for interest gives you a little more breathing room in funding your other expenses. This applies to everything from loans, credit cards and even insurance.

Brand New Toyota Camry
$23,000
66 Month Term

Person A
Credit Score: 730
Interest Rate: 1.99%
Payment: $368.22
Total Interest Paid $1302.39
Total Payments: $24,302.39

Person B
Credit Score: 599
Interest Rate: 14.99%
Payment: $513.97
Total Interest Paid $10,921.44
Total Payments: $33,921.44

Person B pays

$9,616.05 MORE

than person A for the exact same car and price!

This same thing happens with your credit cards, mortgage, loans, etc.

Cleaning up your credit will lower your bills
and can save hundreds of thousands of dollars!

3. Higher approval rate

Whether it's for mortgage or higher credit card limits, or even business loans – a good score states that you are a sound financial investment and is worthy of getting approved.

It's also easier to get pre-approval with a high credit score.

Note that with a passable credit score, you can still get approved, but for a lesser amount.

4. **Get a pass on security deposits**

This applies to utilities, including mobile phone contracts. Depending on your provider, you can even get a discounted price on your phone unit.

DID YOU KNOW? When you apply for a utility service, or transfer the service to a different location, a good credit score saves you from paying a security deposit.

5. **Lifestyle transformation**

This is the summary of all the amazing benefits resulting from your good credit score. If you think about it, your responsible attitude on your finances and hard work on maintaining your obligations are more than enough to get you rewarded.

If you have reached this point – congratulations! You deserve your financial success and I hope you take advantage of the new opportunities that are opening up for you and your loved ones.

CHAPTER 11

Free & Proven Letter Templates

605B IDENTITY THEFT LETTER

Once you've filed a report to the Federal Trade Commission and the local authorities, use this letter to resolve your identity theft issue with the bureaus. Visit Chapter 9 for a refresher.

{client_first_name} {client_last_name}

{client_address}

{bdate}

{ss_number}

{bureau_address}

{curr_date}

Dear Sir/Madam:

I am contacting you about the compromising of my social security number. I am a victim of Identity Theft. I contacted the Federal Trade Commission and filed a complaint # and contacted the police department and obtained an notarize affidavit report # which both are attached. Please block and remove all information from my credit report and send me an updated copy of my credit report. The following items do not belong to me and is a result of fraud that I did not authorize:

{dispute_item_and_explanation}

Please block and remove all information resulting from Identity Theft pursuant to FCRA 605B (15 U.S.C. & 1681 c-2) which states that these accounts must be removed within 4 Business Days of receipt.

Also, please send an updated copy of my credit report to the above address. According to the act, there shall be no charge for this updated report. I also request that you please send notices of corrections to anyone who received my credit report in the past six months.

Sincerely,

{client_signature}

____

{client_first_name} {client_last_name}

609 DISPUTE LETTER

This is our basic dispute letter template. Visit Chapter 4 for a refresher.

{bureau_address}

{curr_date}

To Whom It May Concern,

This letter is a formal complaint that you are reporting inaccurate and incomplete credit information.

According to the Fair Credit Reporting Act, Section 609 (a)(1)(A), you are required by federal law to verify, through the physical verification of the original signed consumer contract, any and all accounts that you post on a credit report. Otherwise anyone paying for your reporting services could fax, mail or email in a fraudulent account.

I demand to see verifiable proof (i.e.: an original consumer contract with my signature on it) that you have on file for the account listed below.

Your failure to positively verify these accounts has hurt my ability to obtain credit. Under the FCRA, unverifiable accounts must be removed and if you are unable to provide me a copy of verifiable proof, you must remove the account listed below.

I demand that the following account be verified or removed immediately:

{dispute_item_and_explanation}

In addition, please remove all non-account holding inquiries over 30 days old.

Under federal law, you have thirty (30) days to complete your re-investigation. Be advised that the description of the procedure used to determine the accuracy and completeness of the information is hereby requested as well, to be provided within fifteen (15) days of the completion of your re-investigation.

Thank you,

{client_first_name} {client_last_name}

{client_signature} {curr_date}

611 DISPUTE LETTER (PART 1)

This is our more powerful dispute letter template. Visit Chapter 4 for a refresher.

{curr_date}

{bureau_name}

{bureau_address}

To Whom It May Concern:

I have been recently informed that there is negative information reported by

{dispute_item_and_explanation}

In the file, you maintained under my so security number. Upon reviewing a copy of my credit report, I see your entry list. I challenge the accuracy, compliance and report the ability of this listing.

Please validate this information and provide with me the copies of any documentation associated with this account, bearing my signature.

In the absence of any such documentation bearing my signature. I formally request that this information be immediately deleted from the credit file you maintain under my Social Security number.

Please note that you have 30 days to complete this investigation, as per the Fair Credit Reporting Act Section 611 (a)(1)(A), and I am keeping a careful record of your actions, including your Method of Verification. I do not consent to e-oscar or any means of automated verification.

Failure to respond satisfactorily within 30 days of receipt of this certified letter may result in a small claims action against your company, seeking $1000 per violation for:

1.) Defamation

2.) Negligent Enablement of Identity Fraud

3.) Violations of the Fair Credit Reporting Act

My contact information is as follows:

{client_first_name} {client_last_name}

{client_address}

{t_no}

P.S. Please be aware that dependent upon your response, I may be detailing any potential issues with your company via an online public press release, including documentation of any potential small claims action.

Cc: Consumer Financial Protection Bureau

Cc: Attorney General's Office

Cc: Better Business Bureau

Thank you,

{client_signature}

{client_first_name} {client_last_name}

{client_address}

{t_no}

{ss_number}

{bdate}

611 DISPUTE LETTER (PART 2)

This is another version of our powerful dispute letter template. Visit Chapter 4 for a refresher.

{bureau_name}

{bureau_address}

{curr_date}

To Whom It May Concern:

This letter is in response to your recent claim that the following has verified that the account they are reporting under my name is accurate:

{dispute_item_and_explanation}

Be advised that the description of the procedure used to determine the accuracy and completeness of the information is hereby requested,

to be provided within fifteen (15) days of the completion of your re-investigation.

Additionally, please provide the name, address, and telephone number of each person contacted regarding this alleged account. I am formally requesting a copy of any documents provided bearing my signature, showing that I have a legally binding contractual obligation to pay them the exact amount claimed.

Any automated response or e-Oscar verification is unacceptable. I am requesting a reinvestigation AND your Method of Verification.

Be aware that I am making a final goodwill attempt to have you clear up this matter. The listed item is entirely inaccurate and incomplete and represents a very serious error in your reporting.

I am maintaining a careful record of my communications with you for the purpose of filing a complaint with the Consumer Financial Protection Bureau and the Attorney General's office, should you continue in your non-compliance. I further remind you that, as in Wenger v. Trans Union Corp., No. 95-6445 (C.D.Cal. Nov. 14, 1995), you may be liable for your willful non-compliance.

Failure to respond satisfactorily within 30 days of receipt of this certified letter may result in a small claims action against your company, seeking $1,000 per violation for:

1.) Defamation

2.) Negligent Enablement of Identity Fraud

3.) Violations of the Fair Credit Reporting Act

My contact information is as follows:

{client_first_name} {client_last_name}

{client_address}

{t_no}

P.S. Please be aware that depending upon your response, I may be detailing any potential issues with your company via an online public press release, including documentation of any potential small claims action.

Cc: Consumer Financial Protection Bureau

Cc: Attorney General's Office

Cc: Better Business Bureau

Thank you,

{client_first_name} {client_last_name}

{client_signature} {curr_date}

BANKRUPTCY LETTER

Use this letter template to dispute a bankruptcy from the bureaus. Visit Chapter 4 for a refresher.

{client_first_name} {client_last_name}

{client_address}

{bdate}

{ss_number}

{curr_date}

To Whom It May Concern:

I looked at online and was not successful at retrieving any information from this public record.

{dispute_item_and_explanation}

Please Investigate and delete from my credit report.

By the provisions of the Fair Credit Reporting Act, I demand that these items be investigated and removed from my report. It is my understanding that you will recheck these items with the creditor who has posted them. Please remove any information that the creditor cannot verify. I understand that under 15 U.S.C Sec. 1681i(a). you must complete this reinvestigation within 30 days of receipt of this letter.

Please DELETE ALL OLD ADDRESSES AND VARIATIONS OF NAMES THAT DO NOT MATCH MY PROOF OF RESIDENCE.

Thank you,

{client_first_name} {client_last_name}

BANKRUPTCY LETTER TO THE COURTS

This is the bankruptcy letter template you can send to the court after the bureau responded to your initial bankruptcy letter to them.

{curr_date}

To Whom It May Concern,

I have a bankruptcy showing on my credit report. I asked the credit bureau to validate the information and they stated they verified with you the information is accurate with you. Can you please confirm that your office reported this bankruptcy to the credit bureau? I was not aware that the U.S. Courts reported information with the with credit bureaus.

Thank you,

{client_first_name} {client_last_name}

BANKRUPTCY LETTER TO THE BUREAUS (WITH RESPONSE FROM THE COURTS)

Once the court replies to you on the bankruptcy letter you sent them, send this letter back to the bureau (where your bankruptcy is at). Don't forget to include the response from the court.

{bureau_name}

{bureau_address}

{curr_date}

To Whom It May Concern,

I have previously disputed the following inaccurate information:

- *Chapter 7/ Chapter 13 Bankruptcy; Docket {account_number}*

In response you verified the items as accurate stating that you have VERIFIED the information with the court. I contacted the court and their response is enclosed.

It is clear they DO NOT REPORT to you or any credit bureau for that matter; therefore, your original response verifying the item with the court was either an error or a lie.

Either way the reporting requirements do not comply with FAIR CREDIT REPORTING ACT 611 (15 U.S.C. 1681I) and the information must be deleted immediately.

Failure to respond satisfactorily within 30 days of receipt of this certified letter may result in a small claims action against your company, seeking $1,000 per violation for:

1.) Defamation

2.) Negligent Enablement of Identity Fraud 3.) Violations of the Fair Credit Reporting Act

P.S. Please be aware that dependent upon your response, I may be detailing any potential issues with your company via an online public press release, including documentation of any potential small claims action.

Cc: Consumer Financial Protection Bureau

Cc: Attorney General's Office

Cc: Better Business Bureau

Sincerely,

{client_first_name} {client_last_name}

{ss_number}

{client_address}

INQUIRY REMOVAL LETTER

To dispute an inquiry, use this letter template. Visit **Chapter 4** for a refresher.

{client_first_name} {client_last_name}

{client_address}

{bureau_name}

{bureau_address}

Date: {curr_date}

RE: Social Security Number: {ss_number}

To Whom It May Concern,

While checking my most recent credit report, I noticed credit inquiries that I did not authorize, made by the following companies:

Inquiries:

I did not authorize anyone employed by these companies to make any inquiry and view my credit report. This is a violation of the Fair Credit Reporting Act Section 1681b(c) and a serious breach of my privacy rights.

Please validate this information with these companies and provide me with copies of any documentation associated with these accounts bearing my signature, authorizing an inquiry. In the absence of any such documentation bearing my signature, I formally request that these fraudulent inquiries be immediately deleted from the credit file that you maintain under my Social Security number.

Please note that you have 30 days to complete this investigation, as per the Fair Credit Reporting Act section 611.

My contact information is as follows:

{dispute_item_and_explanation}

{client_signature}

{client_first_name} {client_last_name}

{ss_number}

{client_address}

FILE UPDATE LETTER

To update your personal information on your credit report, or if you need to remove your old addresses, use this letter template. Visit **Chapter 4** for a refresher.

{bureau_name}
{bureau_address}
{curr_date}

To Whom It May Concern:

I am writing to update/correct my personal information on file with your company.

Please update my address to: {client_address}. This is the only address that should show on my credit report.

Please update my name to: {client_first_name} {client_last_name}. This is the only name that should show on my credit report.

My Last 4 of my SSN: {ss_number}.

My only and correct Date of Birth is {bdate}.

My only telephone is {t_no}. I do not wish to have any other telephone numbers on my credit report.

Please remove all the other addresses off my credit report as they are not deliverable to me by the U.S. post office. They are not reportable as per the FCRA since they are inaccurate. Therefore, it must be removed immediately.

FREEZE LETTER

Use this template to send a security freeze to the 3 major bureaus and the other 6 smaller ones. Visit Chapter 7 for a refresher.

<Company Name>

<Street Address>

<City, State, Postcode>

To Whom It May Concern

I'm writing to you to put a security freeze on my credit report. Under the Fair Credit Report Act you're required to comply. My information is clearly shown below:

Full Name: <First Name>, <Last Name>

Social Security Number: <SSN>

Current Address: <Current Address>

Previous Address: <Only Include If You Moved In The Last 2 Years>

Primary Contact Number: <Primary Contact Number>

Please find enclosed, a legible copy of my Social Security Card and current valid Driver's License showing my current address and date of birth.

After this credit freeze has been filed, can you also please send me written confirmation to the address listed above.

Kind regards,

<First Name>, <Last Name>

<Signature>

<Date signed>

CHAPTER 12

9 Things To Check Before Going For Funding

Majority of what we learned in the previous chapters are the core of how you can get approved for funding. For a refresher, revisit Chapter 1 and Chapter 2.

The principles behind those chapters will help you understand what lenders are looking at on your report, and what you can do to make sure you look good from their point of view.

If you're going to get funding, don't set yourself up for disappointment. Follow my checklist to improve your chances of getting approved:

1. **Check that fraud alerts are removed**

Contrary to what most people say, fraud alerts can get you denied. That's the truth of it. Even if they call you up to verify your identity and you get approved, it's going to be for a lower amount.

Before even thinking of filling up that bank application, make sure to get your fraud alerts removed. It's free.

2. **Check for derogatory accounts**

Plain and simple. You shouldn't have any derogatory accounts before going for funding. Dispute them first to increase your approval rate.

3. **Check your payment history**

You should not have any late payments within the last 2-3 years. If you do, you're going to get low limits, or worse – you won't get approved.

4. **Check your credit card utilization**

Always get a fresh credit report to see your updated utilization to see what adjustments you need to make before you make your trip to the bank. This is key.

5. **Check the age of your credit**

Make sure your age is 6 years or more. If this is going to be a problem, I have outlined solutions in Chapter 6 and Chapter 8 (tradelines!).

6. **Check how many accounts you have**

Make sure you have 3 primaries and 2 authorized users before you get started and that they're showing up on all 3 bureaus.

7. **Check what types of accounts you have**

My advice is to have 5 revolving accounts, 3 primaries and 2 authorized users.

8. **Check the number of inquiries you have**

Make sure this is low. Once you get to 8 or 9, you are less likely to get approved. Chapter 6 will save you here again.

9. **Check your personal information**

If your personal information isn't updated on all three bureaus, it is important to follow the steps I've outlined here.

Before you apply for any credit product, call the institution first and tell them exactly what you plan on getting, then ask what bureau they pull their report from. It is crucial that you tell them exactly what product you plan on getting so they give you the right reporting agency they use for that product.

An example is if you get a credit card from Navy Federal, they pull from TransUnion. But if you get a loan from them, they pull from Equifax.

The reason you're asking for this is when you're filling up their application form, you want to use the personal information that's written on that specific bureau's report. If you have Jon B. Smith in one bureau, and Jonathan Smith in another, you'll want to make sure your application form matches the information from the bureau they're pulling from. This goes the same for the address – you have to write it the exact way it's written on the relevant credit report.

This is a band-aid solution if you really need to open a new account, but I still suggest to fix your personal information in all credit bureaus to make sure they match.

CHAPTER 13

How To Get 10k To 150k In Funding

Now that we've discussed how to prepare you for funding, I want to share with you one key knowledge:

Your good credit score will ONLY get you approved.

"Only?" I'm not making it sound like getting approved is a minor accomplishment because it's not – it's probably the single biggest step in getting funding and it takes hard work to get there.

What I'm trying to say is: while your credit score might get you there, it doesn't necessarily dictate the quality of your loan. Now that you're taking all the steps to get approved – working hard to get to your destination – wouldn't it be better if you can maximize HOW MUCH you're getting approved for?

Yes, take that in. *How much you're getting approved for.* It's one of the most overlooked factors when people are trying to get approved, but it's also one that you should be preparing for so you can manage your expectations.

Here are the other variables that banks or lenders are looking for when determining what loan amount or credit limit they'll give you:

1. **Your existing credit limit**

Lenders are only going to grant you limits that are close to what your revolving credit limit is.

TIP: Seasoned tradelines or becoming an authorized user (from a family member with amazing credit) can help you get around this since a positive account history is going to be added to your report with a potentially higher limit than you have.

2. **Your annual income**

Your income has a big effect on funding. It dictates how big lenders can loan you based on how much you can afford to pay. Simply put, a bigger income is almost synonymous to a bigger loan.

3. **Work history**

Credible employment history = stability. Lenders are more likely to favor you if they know that you can consistently pay off your debt.
A one-year job history is more likely to get you less than if you have over two years of consistent work under your belt.

4. **Average age of all accounts**

This is something we discussed in detail way back in Chapter 1, under "Credit History" and Chapter 2, under "Length of Credit History."
If institutions can see that you have a long (and good!) credit history, they see you as less risky because constantly getting approved for credit means you are financially responsible. This is very self-explanatory, which is why it's also easy to overlook.
If you have a thin credit history, make sure to check out our tip at the end of Chapter 6 to see what you can do to mitigate this.

DID YOU KNOW? Banks tend to ask for stricter documentation if you are self-employed compared to working as an employee. Some of the required documents are tax returns, 4506-T, Profit & Loss Statement, or Balance Sheet. If you are an employee, you would usually just need to produce a pay stub or a W-2.

GOOD INSTITUTIONS FOR FUNDING

1. Credit Unions

Smaller credit unions are most likely to take a personal approach in evaluating your application. Apart from that, they offer lower interest rates.

You will still need to meet certain qualifications to be a member, it's generally very easy to get in.

TIP: Use this online portal to search for credit unions in your area: https://mapping.ncua.gov/

2. Navy Federal

You need a family member (e.g. sibling) or a sponsor to get you in. You can also get in if you are a household member – which means you are added as an authorized user and you are living in the same house as the primary cardholder (same billing address).

They also run a special promotion once a year where they let anyone join (even if they're not military). You can visit their website for more details on this, but once you see more commercials on TV and radio, that's a good time to check.

My favorite card from them is Cash Rewards. As the name states, its biggest perk is its cash back feature. Those rewards don't expire and you can also choose where to use the rewards you accumulate as soon as you earn them. I put mine in my savings account or in the stock market, then never have to worry about it again.

Check Cash Rewards here: **https://www.navyfederal.org/loans-cards/credit-cards/cash-rewards.html**

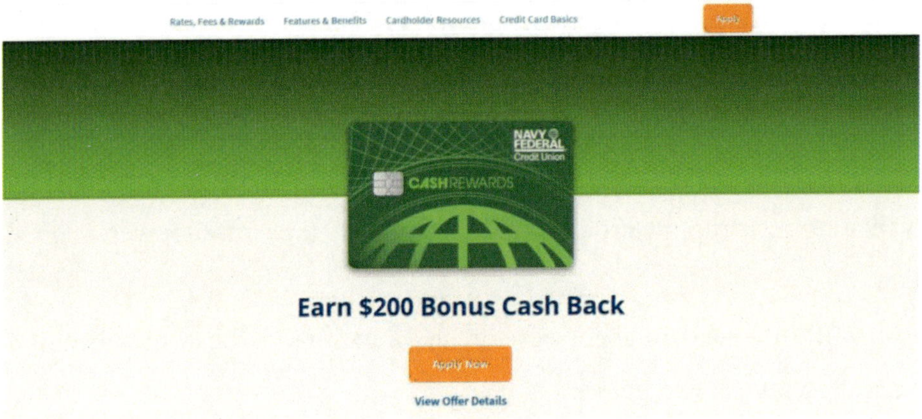

You can check their website here: **https://www.navyfederal.org/**

3. **PenFed**

The Federal Pentagon Credit Union is a good credit union, but like Navy Federal – it has the same member eligibility considerations (like having an immediate family member already enrolled).

One workaround if you want to qualify for PenFed is to sign up with one of their partners. Being a volunteer for the American Red Cross is one of the most used methods.

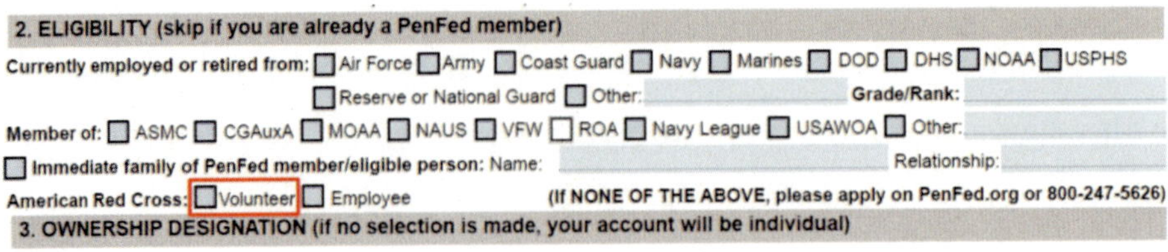

PenFed membership form can be seen here:
https://www.penfed.org/content/dam/penfedbtp/pdfs/13.pdf

ATTENTION: Make it a point to check each of these providers' website for the latest offerings or forms since all products/terms mentioned are the current ones at the time of writing this book.

HOW TO GET A CREDIT LIMIT INCREASE

1. Wait 60 days.
2. Make sure all your cards are within 30% utilization.
3. Ask for an increase every 3-6 months. Some banks are able to provide you one within three months, some within six. Ask for their terms.

TIP: Remember my tip from the previous chapter? Always ask what bureau where your lender is pulling from for each product you're applying for. Lenders may use different bureaus for each product, for example – they may pull from TransUnion for credit card applications, and use Equifax for loans. It's good to check these so you are prepared. Refer back to the previous chapter if you want a refresher.
Another way to see where lenders are pulling from is by visiting Credit Boards, here: https://creditboards.com/forums/#.

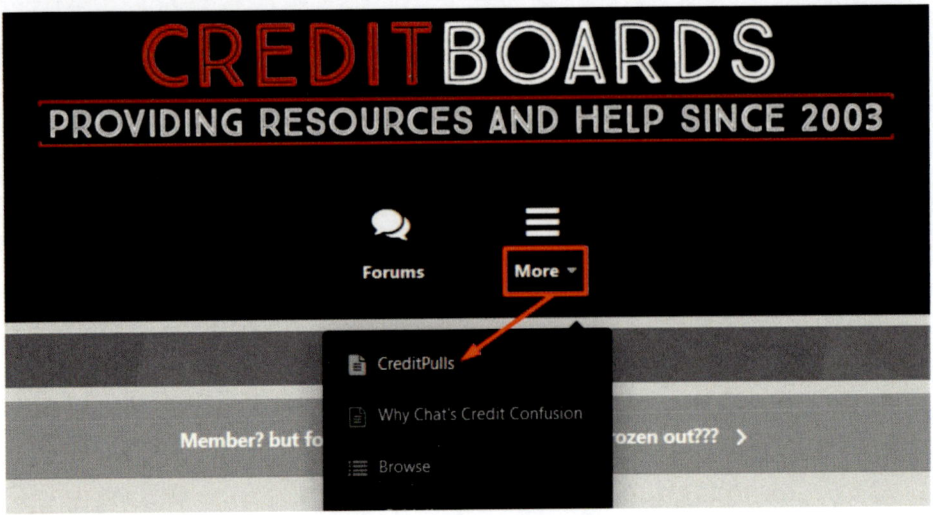

From the "Credit Pulls" section of their forums, you can see how much people are getting approved for, and which bureau the lender is pulling from. Just remember to check the dates to make sure that the information isn't outdated.

Another key knowledge I want to give you is that: once you get approved in one bank, it's not hard to get approved from the rest. I personally have 10 bank accounts, and have credit with each of those lenders (and I pay them on time!). Banks will allow you to get 2 products (I usually go for credit cards and lines of credit).

If you own a business, you can also apply for personal and business products, so that takes you up to 4 credit products.

Using this method can easily get you up to $80,000 if you get approved for two 10k products in four different credit institutions. However, take note of two things:

1. Only borrow what you need so you don't accumulate too much debt,
2. Be responsible in paying off your debt in a timely manner.

Being financially responsible is a long-term investment in yourself so make sure to look at the bigger picture, and don't go for funding for just the short-term gain.

As a final encouragement - you don't have to be 100% on each of the criteria I mentioned to get funding. The key here is to NOT have any derogatory accounts on the bureau that the credit institution is pulling from, which is why it's important to know what bureau they're pulling from for the exact product you're applying for – I can't emphasize on this enough.

I wish you luck on your next funding journey, and I hope this chapter gets you to where you need to be financially!

Thank You

I have enjoyed writing this book and if I have helped you get closer to your financial goals – then this book has served its purpose.

This book is another channel for me to enact my company's mission, "To help fellow Americans achieve financial freedom" because I want to spread credit education to people who can't afford it – which was me at one point in my life.

Thank you again for picking up this book and putting your trust in me.

If you still have doubts about fixing your own credit, I'd be more than happy to give you a free consultation to get you going: **https://www.smithfinancialsllc.com/freecon**

If you want to take the information in this book further to start your own credit coaching / repair business:

1. Check out my masterclass called the **Credit Coaching Blueprint** for more insider strategies, business scalability, hiring and marketing of your credit coaching / repair business: **https://www.creditcoachingblueprint.com**
2. Subscribe to Credit Repair Cloud, the dispute software my company uses. You can get it on 30-day free trial, **here**. You can even use this for your personal disputes!

About the Author

Carlos D. Smith

CEO, Smith Financials LLC

Carlos is a successful entrepreneur, credit coach, mentor, author, and most importantly, a loving family man.

His poor background never got in the way of his success. He has found mentors throughout his life to teach him financial skills like taxes, credit, stocks, and real-estate. He took that knowledge and created his legacy - Smith Financials LLC - a business that has helped thousands of people achieve their financial goals.

Carlos loves listening to his clients' dreams, the ups and downs of their financial life, and how they're working to succeed in life.
Intent on reaching a wider audience, Carlos wrote this book as a guide to anyone looking to increase their credit score and live a blissful life.

LinkedIn: **@carlosdsmith**
Facebook: **@thecreditgod**
Instagram: **@the_credit_god**

Acknowledgement

First of all, I want to thank God for giving me a purpose. Serving people who need financial assistance is a both a privilege and a responsibility that I'm proud of.

Then I want to thank my family who has stood by me and my crazy journey and long hours of preparing this book. Jewel Smith, my wife. My mother, Margarite Wilkes, for helping to keep the kids in line. My Grandmothers Augustine Smith and Elizabeth Wilkes-Mason for always pushing me to be better and holding me to higher standards. To my Uncle Reginald Smith for teaching me how to value money and being a stand-up person. My kids Carly Kimble, Carria Smith, Carlos Smith Jr, Cayla Smith – they're the reason I strive so hard so I can leave them a future.

I would also like to thank the SMITH FINANCIALS LLC Team and Toys De Guzman who has helped make this journey a very fun one. I want to give a special shout out to Marvin Smith & Gloria Smith for their friendship and mentorship in credit, and also showing me that writing this book is not as hard as it seems. Special thanks as well to anyone else who has helped me along the way including John Mayfield, my first mentor.

Made in the USA
Coppell, TX
05 November 2026

11315636R00057